IIS Best Practices and Hardening (applies to IIS7.x and 8.x)

Introduction

Just a quick introduction from me. This booklet is the result of years of experience working in a banking environment deploying IIS. This booklet will cover Best Practices and additional security hardening for developing a secure build of IIS 7.x/8.x.

This is intended for IIS administrators who want to improve their knowledge of best practice and securing IIS and can be used as a quick reference.

All trademarks and copyright owners acknowledged.

Table of contents

Introduction 1

Chapter 1 – Base building IIS...4

   1.1   Available Role Services by Category...............................4

      1.1.1   Common HTTP features 5

      1.1.2   Application Development features 6

      1.1.3   Health and Diagnostics features 7

      1.1.4   Security features 9

      1.1.5   Performance features 11

      1.1.6   Management tools..12

1.1.7   FTP Server Features 13

1.1.8   .NET Framework 4.7 14

Chapter 2 – applying best practice settings post base build.........14

2.0.0   Appcmd path...15

2.0.1   Set the processor scheduling 15

2.0.2   Set disks for data/system and logs......................16

2.0.3   Backing up IIS 16

2.0.4   Default document 19

2.0.5   Disk defragmentation..19

2.0.6   HTTP response headers......................................20

2.0.7   Kernel Mode authentication 21

2.0.8   Classic ASP application pool.............................21

2.0.9   Logfile fields 22

2.1.0   Disable non-essential windows services 23

2.1.1   Deployment retail 24

2.1.2   Antivirus settings..26

2.1.3   HTTP Compression directory location...................27

2.1.4   HTTP Static Compression recommended settings 27

2.1.4   HTTP Dynamic Compression recommended
settings 28

2.1.5   ApplicationPoolIdentity 29

2.1.6   Directory Browsing..30

2.1.7   ASP parent paths...30

2.1.7   Default website and default apppool...................30

2.1.8   IP addresses 31

2.1.9   Unlisted ISAPI and Unlisted CGI 31

2.2.0   Handler mapping permissions 32

2.2.1   IIS configuration auditing 32

2.2.2   Windows authentication 33

2.2.3   Configuration isolation....................................33

2.2.4   IISReset...34

2.2.5   C:\InetPub folder...34

2.2.6   Scheduled recycling of apppools........................34

2.2.7   When to use 32 bit or 64 bit apppools................35

2.2.8   Ping 36

2.2.9   Always do load-testing of your websites 36

2.2.10   Configure IIS7 Output caching 37

2.2.11   Handler mappings and modules 37

2.2.12   MIME types..37

Chapter 3 – remediation of common IIS security vulnerabilities..37

3.0.0   Disable client cache for default website 38

3.0.1   Remove server header/X-POWERED-BY/ASP-NET-
VERSION 38

3.0.2   Mitigate Cross Frame scripting vulnerability........39

3.0.3   Secure HTTP Cookies..39

3.0.4   Set HTTP only attribute for Cookies 39

3.0.5   Default content found.......................................40

3.0.6   Inadequate session timeout..............................40

3.0.7   Poodle SSL vulnerability fix(disable SSLv2 and v3
and PCT1.0) 41

Chapter 4 – additional IIS security hardening 42

4.0.0   Request filtering common security settings.........42

4.0.1   Additional Request filtering security settings 45

4.0.2   Dynamic IP restrictions (IIS8.x only).....................47

4.0.3   HTTP Detailed Error Messages...........................47

4.0.4   IIS_IUSRS group and iiswasKey...........................48

4.0.5   Credentials in .config files 48

4.0.6   SCW and SCM...48

4.0.7   Updates and Security patches............................49

Chapter 1 – Base building IIS

The majority of IIS administrators will need to decide what is the minimum number of IIS role services to install. Selecting the minimum number of role services will reduce the attack surface of IIS.

Below I will be detailing the list of IIS role services available and the recommended list of role services for a given build. For ease of installation of these role services I will be using Server Manager in the examples in this book.

First thing after launching Server Manager is to select from the roles available Web Server (IIS) role using the Add Roles button.

After this step we need to keep the focus on Roles so we can select the Add Roles services:

The role services are grouped on category:

1.1   Available Role Services by Category

- Common HTTP features
- Application Development features
- Health and Diagnostics features

- Security features
- Performance features
- Management Tools
- File Transfer Protocol (FTP) Server features

1.1.1 Common HTTP features

These are the following Role Services available under common http features category:

- **Static content** – it is added by default. This is about serving static content such as html pages and image files. Most IIS servers will need this role service added.
- **Default document** – it is added in by default. This gives administrators the option of configuring what default page gets served to the users which don't specify a page in the URL. It is best practice to set one up. The security exposure of using this is low.
- **Directory browsing** - it is added by default. This enables a generated list of files and folders to be displayed when users browse and not specifying a file or URL and the default document is not configured. This has a high vulnerability as hackers can profile your file and folder structure on your web server. The recommendation is to remove this role service.
- **HTTP errors** – it is added by default. This gives you the option of customising the error messages you display to the users. For example you can provide your helpdesk contact details. It is recommended to enable it and then ensure you make the necessary changes to the error pages so hackers cannot profile you server based on the default error pages.

- **HTTP Redirection** – it is added by default. This can be used to redirect the users to a HTTPS page for example. Low to medium vulnerability. If a hacker injects code to exploit this then users can be redirected to a website of their choice which might host malware.
- **WebDav publishing** – it is added by default. This enables the publishing of files to and from a Web Server using HTTP. High vulnerability as it would allow hackers to inject malicious files to your web server. It is recommended this is removed.

1.1.2   Application Development features

These are the following role services available under application development features category:

- **Asp.Net** – it is added by default. This provides the capability to serve asp.net to the server.
  It is based on .Net Framework. It is commonly used nowadays.
- **.NET Extensibility** – It is added by default. Developers can use the familiar ASP.NET extensibility model and rich .NET APIs to build Web server features that are just as powerful as those written using the native C++ APIs. Use only if required.
- **ASP** – Not added by default. Legacy Microsoft programming standard allowing VBScript and Jscript programming. Hardly anyone uses it anymore.
- **CGI** – Common Gateway Interface (CGI) defines how a Web server passes information to an external program. Typical uses might include using a Web form to collect information and then passing that information to a CGI script to be e-mailed somewhere else. Because CGI is a

standard, CGI scripts can be written by using a variety of programming languages. The downside to using CGI is the performance overhead. It is recommended it is not used.

- **ISAPI Extensions** – Internet Server Application Programming Interface (ISAPI) Extensions provides support for dynamic Web content development using ISAPI extensions. An ISAPI extension runs when requested, just like any other static HTML file or dynamic ASP file. Since ISAPI applications are compiled code, they are processed much faster than ASP files or files that call COM+ components. Use only if required and enable only the strict necessary ones. ISAPI extensions should be replaced by modules as it's legacy feature from IIS6.
- **ISAPI Filters** – Internet Server Application Programming Interface (ISAPI) Filters provides support for Web applications that use ISAPI filters. ISAPI filters are files that can extend or change the functionality provided by IIS. An ISAPI filter reviews every request made to the Web server, until the filter finds one that it needs to process. It can slow down your server. Use only if required. In majority of scenarios this shouldn't be needed.
- **Server-Side Includes** – Server Side Includes (SSI) is a scripting language that is used to generate HTML pages dynamically. The script runs on the server before the page is delivered to the client and typically involves inserting one file into another. For example, you might create an HTML navigation menu and use SSI to dynamically add it to all pages on a Web site. Use only as required.

1.1.3   Health and Diagnostics features

These are the following role services available under health and diagnostics features category:

- **HTTP Logging** – It is added by default. Logs website activity usually when a HTTP transaction occurs. It is usually needed by all IIS servers.
- **Logging Tools** – It is added by default. Provides the infrastructure to manage HTTP logging.
  It is usually not needed. This is adds a scriptable object for parsing log files. Use only if you want to use scripts to parse the log files.
- **Request Monitor** – It is added by default. Request Monitor provi des infrastructure to monitor Web application health by capturing information about HTTP requests in an IIS worker process. Administrators and developers can use Request Monitor to understand which HTTP requests are executing in a worker process when the worker process has become unresponsive or very slow. It is usually needed.
- **Tracing** – Tracing provides infrastructure to diagnose and troubleshoot Web applications. By using failed request tracing, you can troubleshoot difficult to capture events like poor performance or authentication-related failures. This feature buffers trace events for a request and only flushes them to disk if the request falls into a user-configured error condition. It is recommended that this gets enabled on demand only and as soon as the troubleshooting sessions ends it is recommended to be disabled.
- **Custom Logging** – Custom Logging provides support for logging Web server activity in a format that differs greatly from how IIS generates log files. Use Custom Logging to create your own logging module. Custom logging modules are added to IIS by registering a new COM component

that implements ILogPlugin or ILogPluginEx. Enable it only if needed.

- **ODBC Logging** – ODBC Logging provides infrastructure that supports logging Web server activity to an ODBC-compliant database. By using a logging database, you can programmatically display and manipulate data from the logging database on an HTML page. You might do this to search logs for specific events that you want to monitor. Enable only if needed.

1.1.4   Security features

These are the following role services available under Security features category:

- **Basic Authentication** – Not enabled by default. Basic Authentication offers strong browser compatibility. Appropriate for small internal networks, this authentication method is rarely used on the public Internet. Its major disadvantage is that it transmits passwords across the network in the clear. If intercepted, these passwords are simple to decipher. You need to use it in conjunction with SSL to prevent network snooping of passwords.
- **Windows Authentication** – Not enabled by default. This authentication scheme allows administrators in a Windows domain to take advantage of the domain infrastructure for authenticating users. Do not use Windows authentication if users who must be authenticated access your Web site from behind firewalls and proxy servers. Also known as Integrated Authentication.

- **Digest Authentication** – Not enabled by default. Digest Authentication works by sending a password hash to a Windows domain controller to authenticate users. When you need improved security over Basic authentication, consider using Digest authentication, especially if users who must be authenticated access your Web site from behind firewalls and proxy servers.
- **Client Certificate Mapping Authentication** – Not enabled by default. Client Certificate Mapping Authentication uses client certificates to authenticate users. A client certificate is a digital ID from a trusted source. IIS offers two types of authentication using client certificate mapping. This type uses Active Directory to offer one-to-one certificate mappings across multiple Web servers.
- **IIS Client Certificate Mapping Authentication** – Not enabled by default. IIS Client Certificate Mapping Authentication uses client certificates to authenticate users. A client certificate is a digital ID from a trusted source. IIS offers two types of authentication using client certificate mapping. This type uses IIS to offer one-to-one or many-to-one certificate mapping, and offers better performance over Client Certificate Mapping authentication.
- **URL Authorization** – Not enabled by default. URL Authorization allows you to create rules that restrict access to Web content. You can bind these rules to users, groups, or HTTP header verbs. By configuring URL authorization rules, you can prevent users who are not members of certain groups from accessing content or interacting with Web pages.
- **Request Filtering** – Enabled by default. Request Filtering screens all incoming requests to the server and filters these requests based on rules set by the administrator. Many malicious attacks share common characteristics,

such as very long URLs, or requests for an unusual action. By filtering requests, you can try to reduce the impact of these types of attacks. This is the preferred way of replacing URLScan to harden the IIS server. Highly recommended.

- **IP Security** – Not enabled by default. IP and Domain Restrictions allow you to enable or deny content based on the originating IP address or domain name of the request. Instead of using groups, roles, or NTFS file system permissions to control access to content, you can specify IP addresses or domain names. It is one of the best practices to enable and configure this role service to provide another layer of security.

1.1.5   Performance features

These are the following role services available under Performance features category:

- **Static Content Compression** – Enabled by default. Static Content Compression provides infrastructure to configure HTTP compression of static content. This provides more efficient use of bandwidth. Unlike dynamic responses, compressed static responses can be cached without degrading CPU resources. Recommended according to best practices.
- **Dynamic Content Compression** – Not enabled by default. Dynamic Content Compression provides infrastructure to configure HTTP compression of dynamic content. Enabling dynamic compression always gives you more efficient use of bandwidth, but if your server's processor utilization is already very high, the CPU load imposed by dynamic

compression might make your site perform more slowly. This is recommended to be enabled as best practice.

1.1.6 Management tools

These are the role services under this category:

- **IIS management console** – Enabled by default. IIS Manager provides infrastructure to manage IIS by using a graphical user interface. You can use IIS Manager to manage a local or remote Web server that runs IIS.
- **IIS Management Scripts and Tools** – Not enabled by default. IIS Management Scripts and Tools provide infrastructure to manage an IIS server programmatically by using commands in a command prompt window or by running scripts. You can use these tools when you want to automate commands in batch files or when you do not want to incur the overhead of managing IIS by using the graphical user interface.
- **Management Service** – Not enabled by default. Management Service allows the IIS user interface, IIS Manager, to be managed for remote management in IIS. Enable only if needed. Can be exploited by hackers so probably best not to enable it especially on servers hosted in the DMZ.
- **IIS 6.0 Management Compatibility** – Not enabled for default. IIS 6.0 Management Compatibility provides forward compatibility for your applications and scripts that use Admin Base Object (ABO) and Active Directory Service Interface (ADSI) APIs. This lets you use existing IIS 6.0 scripts to manage an IIS 7.x/8.x Web server. Use only if required. Can be exploited by hackers so probably best not to enable it especially on servers hosted in the DMZ.

- **IIS Metabase Compatibility** – Not enabled by default. IIS 6.0 Metabase Compatibility provides infrastructure to query and configure the metabase so that you can run applications and scripts written in earlier versions of IIS that used the Admin Base Object (ABO) or Active Directory Service Interface (ADSI) APIs. Use only if required.
- **IIS 6 WMI Compatibility** – Not enabled by default. IIS 6.0 WMI Compatibility provides Windows Management Instrumentation (WMI) scripting interfaces to programmatically manage and automate tasks for IIS 7.5 by using a set of scripts that you create in the WMI provider. You can manage sites with this service by using the WMI CIM Studio, WMI Event Registration, WMI Event Viewer, and WMI Object Browser tools.
- **IIS 6 Scripting Tools** – Not enabled by default. IIS 6.0 Scripting Tools provides the ability to continue using IIS 6.0 scripting tools that were built to manage IIS 6.0 in IIS 7.x/8.x. This is especially useful if your applications and scripts use ActiveX Data Objects (ADO) or Active Directory Service Interface (ADSI) APIs. IIS 6.0 Scripting Tools requires the WAS Configuration API.
- **IIS 6 Management Console** – Not enabled by default. IIS 6.0 Manager provides infrastructure for administration of remote IIS 6.0 servers.

1.1.7   FTP Server Features

These are the following role services available in this category:

- **FTP Server** – Not enabled by default. FTP Server enables the transfer of files between a client and server by using the FTP protocol. Users can establish an FTP connection and transfer files by using an FTP client or FTP-enabled Web browser. Not recommended. Best to use a secure FTP server instead.

- **FTP Service** – Not enabled by default. Enables FTP publishing on a Web server. Not recommended. Not sufficiently secure.
- **FTP Extensibility** – Not enabled by default. Enables support for FTP extensibility features such as custom providers, ASP.NET users or IIS Manager users. Not recommended.

The above content has been compiled from Microsoft's Technet from the following URL:

https://technet.microsoft.com/en-us/library/cc753473(v=ws.11).aspx

1.1.8   .NET Framework 4.7

This is currently the latest recommended, highly compatible, version which should be installed on Windows 2008 R2 SP1 upwards. Most IIS implementations would need this installed.

Simply download from the following link below:

https://www.microsoft.com/en-us/download/details.aspx?id=55167

Chapter 2 – applying best practice settings post base build

Now after finalising the base build it's a good time to apply the best practice settings to IIS. Also if you are running IIS in a high volume PRODUCTION environment it is recommended that IIS is installed on a dedicated server not collocated with SQL server or Exchange.

2.0.0   Appcmd path

To make things easier as we need to apply quite a few appcmd commands for various settings we should add appcmd in default path. Open an elevated (run as administrator) command prompt (all the appcmd commands in this book should be run like this) window and run the following command:

SETX PATH "%PATH%;%WINDIR%\System32\inetsrv" /M

You might have to reboot your server for changes to take effect. The reason for this is the fact that the path gets added to the computer wide path variable.

2.0.1   Set the processor scheduling

It is best practice that the processor scheduling should be set to background services as IIS runs in the background. It is recommended for production servers.

2.0.2   Set disks for data/system and logs

For production servers you should set different physical disks for data and system and logs. This will improve the performance of the server.

2.0.3   Backing up IIS

Before going further it's a good idea to configure backup for IIS.

Backup the machine.config and root web.config at these paths below:

%WINDIR%\Microsoft.Net\Framework\version no\config\Machine.config and web.config

As well as the above backup administration.config, applicationHost.config and redirection.config at the path below:

WINDIR%\System32\inetsrv

There is also an important appcmd command to backup IIS:

%windir%\system32\inetsrv\appcmd.exe add backup "initial backup"

To restore from backup use the appcmd command below:

%windir%\system32\inetsrv\appcmd.exe restore backup "initial backup"

As well as the above there are also 3 IIS encryption keys which should be backed up:

- *IISWASOnlyRsaProvider/iisWasKey:*
  6de9cb26d2b98c01ec4e9e8b34824aa2_G
  UID

- *AesProvider/iisConfigurationKey:*
  76944fb33636aeddb9590521c2e8815a_G
  UID

- *RsaProtectedConfigurationProvider/NetFr*
  ameworkConfigurationKey:
  d6d986f09a1ee04e24c949879fdb506c_G
  UID

REM To back up the keys of the three providers AesProvider,
IISWASOnlyRsaProvider and RsaProtectedConfigurationProvider:

REM Backup AesProvider/iisConfigurationKey

%WINDIR%\Microsoft.NET\Framework64\version 2
folder\aspnet_regiis -px "iisConfigurationKey"
"%IIS_BACKUPKEY_DIR%\iisConfigurationKey.xml" -pri

REM Backup IISWASOnlyRsaProvider/iisWasKey

%WINDIR%\Microsoft.NET\Framework64\version 2
folder\aspnet_regiis -px "iisWasKey"
"%IIS_BACKUPKEY_DIR%\iisWasKey.xml" –pri

REM Backup
RsaProtectedConfigurationProvider/NetFrameworkConfiguration
Key

%WINDIR%\Microsoft.NET\Framework64\version 2 folder\aspnet_regiis -px "NetFrameworkConfigurationKey" "%IIS_BACKUPKEY_DIR%\NetFrameworkConfigurationKey.xml" – pri

To restore from backup:

REM To restore the keys of the three providers AesProvider, IISWASOnlyRsaProvider and RsaProtectedConfigurationProvider:

REM Restore AesProvider/iisConfigurationKey

%WINDIR%\Microsoft.NET\Framework64\version 2 folder\aspnet_regiis -pi "iisConfigurationKey" "%IIS_BACKUPKEY_DIR%\iisConfigurationKey.xml"

REM Restore IISWASOnlyRsaProvider/iisWasKey

%WINDIR%\Microsoft.NET\Framework64\version 2 folder\aspnet_regiis -pi "iisWasKey" "%IIS_BACKUPKEY_DIR%\iisWasKey.xml"

REM Restore RsaProtectedConfigurationProvider/NetFrameworkConfigurationKey

%WINDIR%\Microsoft.NET\Framework64\version 2 folder\aspnet_regiis -pi "NetFrameworkConfigurationKey" "%IIS_BACKUPKEY_DIR%\NetFrameworkConfigurationKey.xml"

One last config which needs backing up is the application web.config from the folder where the web application has been deployed.

To increase the number of histories for automatic backup to 10, you can run the following command line from an elevated shell:

REM To increase the configuration history number for automatic backup to 10

%WINDIR%\system32\inetsrv\appcmd.exe set config -section:system.applicationHost/configHistory /maxHistories:10 /commit:apphost

2.0.4   Default document

Set the default document to the appropriate one (based on your application e.g:index.html) and move it to the top of the list. Setting this to your appropriate application default document will improve performance as IIS won't have to iterate through the list of default documents in your list to select the correct document. You should also remove the options you don't use(e.g:iistart.htm)

2.0.5   Disk defragmentation

Probably your windows sysadmins have done this already but it's worth reminding them that the disks should be defragmented regularly.

2.0.6 HTTP response headers

It's best practice to set the HTTP common response headers, to one of the settings explained below, at website level:

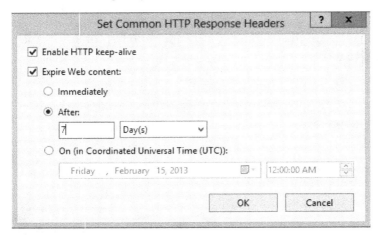

Enable HTTP keep-alive ensures that content is delivered quicker by the server

Expire Web content setting - **After**

sets the amount of time after which the content will be expired. This setting is best for content that is updated regularly, such as on a daily or weekly basis. Type a value in the corresponding box and select one of the following values from the list: **Second(s), Minute(s), Hour(s), Day(s).**

Expire Web content – **On**

sets an exact date and time when the content will expire. This setting is best for content that is not expected to change frequently.

Expire Web content – **Immediately**

expires the content immediately after it is delivered. This setting is best for content that contains sensitive information that you do not want to be cached or that is updated very frequently

2.0.7   Kernel Mode authentication

It is best practice to use Kernel mode authentication whenever possible (for Windows authentication).

These are the advantages of using it:

- Your Web applications can run using lower-privileged accounts.
- If you use Kerberos authentication, you can use a different account than the default account associated with the Service Principle Name (SPN) of the server.

- If you use kernel-mode authentication, you can use the Windows authentication Kerberos provider without performing explicit SPN configuration

2.0.8   Classic ASP application pool

Use the below setting for an ASP classic apppool:

In the Edit Application pool screen set the name and the .Net Framework to No Managed code. Last option on this screen is to set the Managed pipeline mode to Classic.

2.0.9 Logfile fields

Use the below Microsoft recommended fields for W3C format logfiles:

- Date
- Time
- Client
- IP Address
- User Name
- Service Name
- Server Name
- Server IP Address
- Server Port
- Method
- URI Stem
- URI Query
- Protocol Status
- Protocol Substatus
- Win32 Status
- Bytes Sent
- Bytes Received
- Time Taken

2.1.0   Disable non-essential windows services

Disabling windows services which aren't needed on a dedicated web server. Here's an example of a list of services not needed:

- Alerter

- ClipBook

- Computer Browser

- DHCP Client

- DHCP Server

- Fax Service

- File Replication

- INfrared Monitor

- Internet Connection Sharing

- Messenger

- NetMeeting Remote Desktop Sharing

- Network DDE

- Network DDE DSDM

- NWLink NetBIOS

- NWLink IPX/SPX

- Print Spooler

- TCP/IP NetBIOS Helper Service

- Telephony

- Telnet

- Uninterruptible Power Supply

  The list above applies to Windows Server 2003...some of them have been deprecated in 2008 and 2012. Probably best to work with your Windows sysadmin when disabling windows services on your web server but you get the idea.

  Please see the below article which cautions on disabling essential services by mistake:

  http://blogs.technet.com/b/askperf/archive/2008/11/18/disablin g-unnecessary-services-a-word-to-the-wise.aspx

2.1.1   Deployment retail

To avoid using <compilation debug=true> you can set this in the machine.config:

<configuration>

  <system.web>

```
<deployment retail="true"/>

  </system.web>

</configuration>
```

Compilation debug=true when set has the drawbacks as per below:

1) The compilation of ASP.NET pages takes longer (since some batch optimizations are disabled)

2) Code can execute slower (since some additional debug paths are enabled)

3) Much more memory is used within the application at runtime

4) Scripts and images downloaded from the WebResources.axd handler are not cached

So basically never have compilation debug=true set on PRODUCTION IIS machines.

You can also use these appcmd commands to set deployment retail=true in machine.config:

REM For .Net 4.0 framework 4 x64

```
windir%\system32\inetsrv\appcmd unlock config
/section:system.web/deployment /commit: MACHINE /clr:4.0

%windir%\system32\inetsrv\appcmd set config -
section:system.web/deployment /retail:true /clr:4.0
/commit:MACHINE

windir%\system32\inetsrv\appcmd lock config
/section:system.web/deployment /commit:MACHINE /clr:4.0
```

2.1.2   Antivirus settings

Disable real-time antivirus scan (at least for read operations, if possible). This will prevent the slowing of your IIS server and random access denied errors or apppool recycles. Also keep your antivirus up to date with the latest definitions.

- Exclude at least the following directories:

    - Default folders for x86 and x64 compiled ASP.Net code: *%WINDIR%\Microsoft.NET\Framework\{version}\Temporary ASP.NET* files

    - *%WINDIR%\Microsoft.NET\Framework64\{version}\Temporary ASP.NET* files

    - IIS binaries installation folder: *%WINDIR%\System32\Inetsrv*

    - IIS configuration folder: *%WINDIR%\System32\Inetsrv\Config*

    - Schema for IIS: *%WINDIR%\System32\Inetsrv\Config\Schema*

    - Default content location: *%SYSTEMDRIVE%\Inetpub\wwwroot*

    - Default logging location: *%SYSTEMDRIVE%\Inetpub\Logs*

    - Default history location: *%SYSTEMDRIVE%\Inetpub\History*

    - Default folder for storing compressed content:

> *%SYSTEMDRIVE%\Inetpub\temp\IIS*
> temporary compressed files

- Default folder for compiled ASP templates: *%SYSTEMDRIVE%\Inetpub\temp\ASP* compiled templates

- Default configuration isolation path: *%SYSTEMDRIVE%\Inetpub\temp\appPool s*

Default folder for error pages: *%SYSTEMDRIVE%\Inetpub\custerr*

I would also exclude web.config for the web applications to prevent random recycles of the application pools.

2.1.3   HTTP Compression directory location

This needs to be away from the system drive due to the additional I/O done by the compression.

2.1.4   HTTP Static Compression recommended settings

Given how powerful the servers are nowadays it is possible to set the level of static compression quite high.

For example, this is how you can set the level of compression to 9 using appcmd:

REM To set a level of 9 for static compression :

```
%WINDIR%\system32\inetsrv\appcmd.exe set config
/section:httpCompression
/[name='gzip'].staticCompressionLevel:9
```

These are examples of how you can set the static compression based on CPU level so there isn't a hit on performance.

REM Enabling static compression to kick in below 40% of CPU level

```
%WINDIR%\system32\inetsrv\appcmd.exe set config -section:httpCompression /staticCompressionEnableCpuUsage:40
```

REM How to disable static compression when CPU level gets to 90%

```
%WINDIR%\system32\inetsrv\appcmd.exe set config -section:httpCompression /staticCompressionDisableCpuUsage:90
```

2.1.4   HTTP Dynamic Compression recommended settings

Dynamic compression is not enabled by default. It is recommended you enable it. The examples below are good starting points for setting the level of compression and enabling it and disabling it dynamically based on CPU usage to minimize a performance hit on the server.

REM How to set a compression level of 5 for dynamic compression :

```
%WINDIR%\system32\inetsrv\appcmd.exe set config
/section:httpCompression
/[name='gzip'].dynamicCompressionLevel:5
```

REM Hot to set a dynamic compression below 60% CPU usage

```
%WINDIR%\system32\inetsrv\appcmd.exe set config -
section:httpCompression
/dynamicCompressionEnableCpuUsage:60
```

REM How to set a dynamic compression level to disable at 90% CPU usage

```
%WINDIR%\system32\inetsrv\appcmd.exe set config -
section:httpCompression /staticCompressionDisableCpuUsage:90
```

You need to disable compression for some file formats such as PDF,ZIP and pptx,xlsx,docx as they are already compressed. If you don't ignore them you will end up with a larger file size.

2.1.5   ApplicationPoolIdentity

When using AppPoolIdentity, you have a separate identity for each apppool. This means that you can control the services and securities for your apppool. Therefore, if you have multiple applications using ApplicationPoolIdentity is better as it is more secure.

2.1.6   Directory Browsing

If you enable it users will be able to see the contents of the directories on your server when browsing the root of your website and if you don't set a default document. So, it is advisable to keep this disabled. To disable it at server level please see the appcmd command below:

REM Disabling Directory Browsing option at top level

%WINDIR%\system32\inetsrv\appcmd set config /section:directoryBrowse /enabled:false

2.1.7   ASP parent paths

It is recommended not to use ASP parent paths as a hacker can use double dots to navigate upwards in your directory and upload scripts higher in your directory structure which can then navigate to a folder with elevated privileges(C:\wwwroot\inetpub\scripts, which has Everyone Full Control permission by default, or C:\winnt\system32)

2.1.7   Default website and default apppool

This gets installed by default as an example of a successful IIS installation. It is best to stop it and install your applications in separate websites with dedicated apppools. Hacking tools and utilities are almost always designed to scan default locations to begin their attacks. Also stop the default apppool which gets created by default.

This link to a Microsoft support doc takes you through your options about relocating the default website content:

https://support.microsoft.com/en-us/help/2752331/guidance-for-relocation-of-iis-7.0-and-iis-7.5- content-directories

2.1.8   IP addresses

It is best to use dedicated ip addresses for the websites. Web sites are configured to listen on all unassigned interfaces by default. If there is a system compromise, a hacker may use the local loopback address (localhost, or 127.0.0.1) to find website content and access they wish. Binding the web site to a specific IP address makes it more difficult.

2.1.9   Unlisted ISAPI and Unlisted CGI

It is best to disable these options as a hacker might be able to use malicious ISAPI or CGI scripts. You can use the following appcmd script to disable it:

```
%WINDIR%\system32\inetsrv\appcmd.exe set config -section:system.webServer/security/isapiCgiRestriction /notListedIsapisAllowed:false /notListedCgisAllowed:false
```

2.2.0   Handler mapping permissions

It is recommended not to give Execute or Write permissions to any locations unless absolutely needed. If they are given the scope of that permission needs to be restricted to a specific location. It is also recommended not to give Execute or Script permissions in conjunction with Write permissions for any location.

2.2.1   IIS configuration auditing

This is not enabled by default. It is very useful for keeping track of any config edits which happen on the IIS server. There are two ways of enabling it:

1. From an elevated command prompt:

   wevtutil Set-Log Microsoft-IIS-Configuration/Operational /e:true

   To verify it is enabled:

   wevtutil Get-Log Microsoft-IIS-Configuration/Operational | findstr /C:enabled

2. In Event Viewer browse Application and Services Logs/Microsoft/Windows/IIS-Configuration/Operational and then right-click and pick enable log.

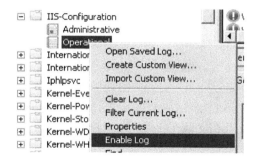

2.2.2 Windows authentication

Use persistence for windows authentication (enabled by default for Kerberos and NTLM in IIS 8.0) to keep auth connection open for next authentication request. This can improve the performance for auth requests.

To enable it use the example below:

appcmd set config /section:windowsAuthentication /authPersistNonNTLM:true

2.2.3 Configuration isolation

By default you have the following setting for apppools and apppool ids and also for config files:

- 1 site - 1 appool - 1 apppoolid - 1 configuration file (location=Registry Key ConfigIsolationPath)

Best practice is to keep this registry key below enabled to maintain the above default config isolation:

HKLM\System\CurrentControlSet\Services\WAS\Parameters\Confi glsolationEnabled=1

- If set as per above it will use a dedicated config file.
- It is not recommended to set this to 0. This will disable config isolation and the worker process will try to read applicationHost.config (Access Control Entry permissions will need to be set)

2.2.4   IISReset

It is best not to use it. All sessions get lost and also the application in memory data is lost as well. Microsoft advises not to use it. Use the recycling of apppools instead.

2.2.5   C:\InetPub folder

DO NOT MOVE TO ANOTHER PARTITION. It is not supported. You can copy it to another partition.

Refer to: http://support.microsoft.com/kb/2752331

2.2.6   Scheduled recycling of apppools

By default this is set for 1740 mins (approx. 29 hours). This is not recommended. If you need to recycle do it at off-peak times when there is little activity on your websites.

To disable the default recycling option for all application pools use the following appcmd script from an elevated command prompt:

REM Setting a non-default recycling policy for all Application Pools

```
%WINDIR%\system32\inetsrv\appcmd.exe set config -
section:system.applicationHost/applicationPools
/applicationPoolDefaults.recycling.periodicRestart.time:"07:00:00
" /commit:apphost
```

To log all recycle events use the following appcmd script:

REM How to set to log all recycling events

```
%WINDIR%\system32\inetsrv\appcmd.exe set config -
section:system.applicationHost/applicationPools
/applicationPoolDefaults.recycling.logEventOnRecycle:ConfigChan
ge,IsapiUnhealthy,Memory,OnDemand,PrivateMemory,Requests,
Schedule,Time /commit:apphost
```


2.2.7   When to use 32 bit or 64 bit apppools

Use 32 bit application pools (even on 64 bit machines)

- Use 32-bit worker processes, for most deployment scenarios:
- Recommended for performance and compatibility

Use 64-bit application pools :

- With applications that require large address space (also which perform caching), or
- If the application is generating OutOfMemory errors (.NET)

Use the default values for other settings:

- For example for Rapid-fail protection option

2.2.8 Ping

This health monitoring option sends a health ping to the worker processes every 30 secs. If no response is received in 90 secs then the worker process of the apppool will be recycled.

It is recommended to keep this default option enabled.

2.2.9 Always do load-testing of your websites

As the title of this point implies best practice is to conduct load-testing of your websites to reveal the potential performance bottlenecks in your applications. The common performance counters are recommended to be monitored during load-testing:

- Windows Server counters:
  System\Processor Queue Length
  Processor\% Processor Time
  PhysicalDisk\% Disk Time
  Network Interface\Bytes Total/sec
  Memory\Available Mbytes
  Memory\Pages/sec
- IIS specific counters:
  .NET CLR Exceptions\# of Exceptions Thrown / sec
  .NET CLR Memory\# Total Committed Bytes
  Web Service\Get Requests/sec
  Web Service\Post Requests/sec
  Web Service\Current Connections
  ASP.NET Applications\Requests/Sec
  ASP.NET\Application Restarts
  ASP.NET\Request Wait Time

ASP.NET\Requests Queued
Web Service\URI Cache Flushes
Web Service\URI Cache Hits
Web Service\URI Cache Hits%
Web Service\URI Cache Misses

2.2.10 Configure IIS7 Output caching

Use caching wherever possible to boost performance.
Please see the below URL on how you can configure:

https://www.iis.net/learn/manage/managing-performance-settings/configure-iis-7-output-caching

2.2.11 Handler mappings and modules

To reduce the attack surface of the webserver use the minimal handler mappings and modules

2.2.12 MIME types

Configure the minimal number of MIME types for your application.

Chapter 3 – remediation of common IIS security vulnerabilities

3.0.0   Disable client cache for default website

Use the example below to disable client cache for default website:

appcmd.exe set config "Default Web Site" -
section:system.webServer/staticContent
/clientCache.cacheControlMode:"DisableCache"

3.0.1   Remove server header/X-POWERED-BY/ASP-NET-VERSION

The following blog describes how to remove unwanted http response headers:

https://blogs.msdn.microsoft.com/varunm/2013/04/23/remo
ve-unwanted-http-response-headers/

Basically follow the step by step instructions below:

Download URL Rewrite matching binary version of the server

1)   Install URL Rewrite msi

2)   View server variables – Add RESPONSE_SERVER

3)   Back to rules. Add Outbound blank rule

4)   Name the rule REMOVE_HEADER

5)   Matching scope server variable – variable name
RESPONSE_SERVER

6)   Pattern .+ and then apply

3.0.2   Mitigate Cross Frame scripting vulnerability

Follow the instructions below to remediate:

- Open Internet Information Services (IIS) Manager.

- In the Connections pane on the left side, expand the **Sites** folder and select the site that you want to protect.

- Double-click the **HTTP Response Headers** icon in the feature list in the middle.

- In the Actions pane on the right side, click **Add**.

- In the dialog box that appears, type **X-Frame-Options** in the **Name** field and type **SAMEORIGIN** in the **Value** field.

Click **OK** to save your changes.

3.0.3   Secure HTTP Cookies

This is a vulnerability as an attacker can obtain the user credentials if not secured with SSL.
Use the following appcmd script from an elevated command prompt to enable secure http cookies:

appcmd.exe set config "Default Web Site" -section:system.web/httpCookies /httpOnlyCookies:"True" /requireSSL:"True"

3.0.4   Set HTTP only attribute for Cookies

Setting the HTTP only attribute for Cookies should reduce cross-site scripting attacks.
To set within the application's web.config use the following:

Add within <system.web> section:

<httpCookies httpOnlyCookies="true" />

3.0.5   Default content found

Delete content found at c:\inetpub\wwwroot\ . Especially iistart.htm.

3.0.6   Inadequate session timeout

To mitigate this follow the instructions below:

Open IIS Manager and navigate to the level you want to manage.

In Features View, double-click Session State.

On the Session State page, in the Session State Mode Settings area, click In process.

(Optional) Configure cookie settings in the Cookie Settings area on the Session State page.

(Optional) Check the Use hosting identity for impersonation check box to use Windows authentication and the host process identity (either ASP.NET or a Windows service identity) for remote connections.

Click Apply in the Actions pane.

3.0.7 Poodle SSL vulnerability fix(disable SSLv2 and v3 and PCT1.0)

If you have enabled SSL on any of your websites you need to disable SSLv2/SSLv3 and PCT1.0. As an aside if you pass confidential data and credentials you always need to enable SSL for your websites. I am not covering this here as I am assuming that you as an administrator of IIS you should be already familiar with installing and configuring SSL certificates. If you are running RDS you shouldn't also disable TLS1.0 as by default RDS uses this to encrypt the communication channel.

For example you can disable SSL v3 as per the following instructions:

Click Start, click Run, type regedit, and then click OK.

In Registry Editor, locate the following registry key:

HKey_Local_Machine\System\CurrentControlSet\Control\Security Providers\SCHANNEL\Protocols\SSL 3.0\Server

Note If the complete registry key path does not exist, you can create it by expanding the available keys and using the New -> Key option from the Edit menu.

On the Edit menu, click Add Value.

In the Data Type list, click DWORD.

In the Value Name box, type Enabled, and then click OK.

Note If this value is present, double-click the value to edit its current value.

In the Edit DWORD (32-bit) Value dialog box, type 0 .

Click OK. Restart the computer.

You can also use the best practices button within this application IIScrypto which you can download from nartac.com and then reboot the server for changes to take effect. This will disable PCT1.0 as well as SSLv3 and SSLv2 as well as disable the insecure cyphers leaving only Triple DES 168, AES 128 and AES 256.

Chapter 4 – additional IIS security hardening

4.0.0   Request filtering common security settings

You can add the below section to applicationhost.config at the bottom of the file. The settings added are easy to determine in the xml:

```
<requestFiltering allowHighBitCharacters="false">
        <fileExtensions allowUnlisted="true"
applyToWebDAV="true">
                <add fileExtension=".asax" allowed="false" />
                <add fileExtension=".ascx" allowed="false" />
                <add fileExtension=".master" allowed="false" />
                <add fileExtension=".skin" allowed="false" />
                <add fileExtension=".browser" allowed="false" />
                <add fileExtension=".sitemap" allowed="false" />
                <add fileExtension=".config" allowed="false" />
                <add fileExtension=".cs" allowed="false" />
                <add fileExtension=".csproj" allowed="false" />
                <add fileExtension=".vb" allowed="false" />
                <add fileExtension=".vbproj" allowed="false" />
                <add fileExtension=".webinfo" allowed="false" />
                <add fileExtension=".licx" allowed="false" />
                <add fileExtension=".resx" allowed="false" />
                <add fileExtension=".resources" allowed="false" />
                <add fileExtension=".mdb" allowed="false" />
```

```
<add fileExtension=".vjsproj" allowed="false" />
<add fileExtension=".java" allowed="false" />
<add fileExtension=".jsl" allowed="false" />
<add fileExtension=".ldb" allowed="false" />
<add fileExtension=".dsdgm" allowed="false" />
<add fileExtension=".ssdgm" allowed="false" />
<add fileExtension=".lsad" allowed="false" />
<add fileExtension=".ssmap" allowed="false" />
<add fileExtension=".cd" allowed="false" />
<add fileExtension=".dsprototype" allowed="false"
/>
<add fileExtension=".lsaprototype" allowed="false"
/>
<add fileExtension=".sdm" allowed="false" />
<add fileExtension=".sdmDocument"
allowed="false" />
<add fileExtension=".mdf" allowed="false" />
<add fileExtension=".ldf" allowed="false" />
<add fileExtension=".ad" allowed="false" />
<add fileExtension=".dd" allowed="false" />
<add fileExtension=".ldd" allowed="false" />
<add fileExtension=".sd" allowed="false" />
<add fileExtension=".adprototype" allowed="false"
/>
<add fileExtension=".lddprototype" allowed="false"
/>
<add fileExtension=".exclude" allowed="false" />
<add fileExtension=".refresh" allowed="false" />
<add fileExtension=".compiled" allowed="false" />
<add fileExtension=".msgx" allowed="false" />
<add fileExtension=".vsdisco" allowed="false" />
<add fileExtension=".rules" allowed="false" />
<add fileExtension=".exe" allowed="false" />
<add fileExtension=".bat" allowed="false" />
<add fileExtension=".com" allowed="false" />
<add fileExtension=".cmd" allowed="false" />
<add fileExtension=".htw" allowed="false" />
<add fileExtension=".ida" allowed="false" />
```

```xml
        <add fileExtension=".idq" allowed="false" />
        <add fileExtension=".htr" allowed="false" />
        <add fileExtension=".idc" allowed="false" />
        <add fileExtension=".shtm" allowed="false" />
        <add fileExtension=".shtml" allowed="false" />
        <add fileExtension=".stm" allowed="false" />
        <add fileExtension=".printer" allowed="false" />
        <add fileExtension=".ini" allowed="false" />
        <add fileExtension=".log" allowed="false" />
        <add fileExtension=".pol" allowed="false" />
        <add fileExtension=".dat" allowed="false" />
    </fileExtensions>
    <verbs allowUnlisted="false" applyToWebDAV="true">
        <add verb="GET" allowed="true" />
        <add verb="HEAD" allowed="true" />
        <add verb="POST" allowed="true" />
        <add verb="PROPFIND" allowed="false" />
        <add verb="PROPPATCH" allowed="false" />
        <add verb="MKCOL" allowed="false" />
        <add verb="DELETE" allowed="false" />
        <add verb="PUT" allowed="false" />
        <add verb="COPY" allowed="false" />
        <add verb="MOVE" allowed="false" />
        <add verb="LOCK" allowed="false" />
        <add verb="UNLOCK" allowed="false" />
        <add verb="OPTIONS" allowed="false" />
        <add verb="SEARCH" allowed="false" />
        <add verb="TRACE" allowed="false" />
    </verbs>
    <hiddenSegments applyToWebDAV="true">
        <add segment="web.config" />
        <add segment="bin" />
        <add segment="App_code" />
        <add segment="App_GlobalResources" />
        <add segment="App_LocalResources" />
        <add segment="App_WebReferences" />
        <add segment="App_Data" />
        <add segment="App_Browsers" />
```

```
      </hiddenSegments>
      <requestLimits>
        <headerLimits>
          <add header="Translate:" sizeLimit="0" />
          <add header="If:" sizeLimit="0" />
          <add header="Lock-Token:" sizeLimit="0" />
          <add header="Transfer-Encoding:" sizeLimit="0"
/>
        </headerLimits>
      </requestLimits>
      <denyUrlSequences>
        <add sequence=".." />
        <add sequence="./" />
        <add sequence="\" />
        <add sequence=":" />
        <add sequence="%" />
        <add sequence="&amp;" />
      </denyUrlSequences>
      <denyQueryStringSequences>
        <add sequence=">" />
        <add sequence="&lt;" />
      </denyQueryStringSequences>
      <alwaysAllowedQueryStrings>
      </alwaysAllowedQueryStrings>
    </requestFiltering>
```

4.0.1   Additional Request filtering security settings

1. **maxAllowedContentLength**
    a. This setting will help with buffer overflow situations. Setting the appropriate option for your application is required.
    b. For example to set this to 20000000 bytes please see the below instructions:
    c. In IIS manager select the site/application you want to apply it to and then select Request

filtering and then edit Feature settings in the action pane.

d. In the section request limits enter the value of 20000000

2. maxURL setting

This sets the length of the URL IIS would accept. Hackers can send long URLs containing unusual sequences so it is recommended to set this option.

Follow the instructions below to set a limit:

a. In IIS manager select the site/application you want to apply it to and then select Request filtering and then edit Feature settings in the action pane.

b. In the section request limits enter the value for maxURL which has been verified as being OK for your application.

3. maxQueryString setting

This sets the length of the query string IIS would accept. Hackers can send long query strings so it is recommended to set a limit for this option.

Follow the instructions below to set a limit:

a. In IIS manager select the site/application you want to apply it to and then select Request filtering and then edit Feature settings in the action pane.

b. In the section request limits enter the value for maxQueryString which has been verified as being OK for your application.

4. Disallow double escaping

This disallows double escaping characters IIS would accept. Hackers can send double escaping sequences in their requests.

Follow the instructions below to set:

    a.   In IIS manager select the site/application you want to apply it to and then select Request filtering and then edit Feature settings in the action pane.

In the General section uncheck Allow Double Escaping.

4.0.2   Dynamic IP restrictions (IIS8.x only)

IIS8.0 introduced this option which can be use to thwart DDOS attacks by blocking excessive repeated access attempts.

You need to add IP and Domain restrictions first. IIS can be configured to to deny access to websites based on the number of times that an HTTP client accesses the server within a specified time interval, or based on the number of concurrent connections from an HTTP client.

Please see the below URL where you can get step by step instructions on how to configure this feature:

https://www.iis.net/learn/get-started/whats-new-in-iis-8/iis-80-dynamic-ip-address-restrictions

4.0.3   HTTP Detailed Error Messages

Showing HTTP detailed error messages to display remotely can give clues as to how your IIS server is configured so it's best to disable it.

Please see the below URL to configure HTTP error messages to not display remotely:

https://www.iis.net/configreference/system.webserver/httperrors

While here you might as well ensure that custom Error messages are enabled.

4.0.4 IIS_IUSRS group and iiswasKey

By default only administrators and system should have access to this encryption key. In addition though IIS_IUSRS has access as well. This is a vulnerability and should be remediated.

For example you can use the below command from an elevated command prompt for .Net 4.0 64 bit:

%systemroot\Windows\Microsoft.NET\Framework64\v4.0.30319 \aspnet_regiis.exe -pr iisWasKey

4.0.5 Credentials in .config files

This is a vulnerability for IIS admin users credentials when stored in machine.config, root level web.config or application web.config files.

To remove please follow the instructions below:

a) Open the above config files and find the <credentials> section.
b) Remove the section

4.0.6 SCW and SCM

Use Security Configuration Wizard and Security Compliance Wizard to check the potential security pitfalls of your server leftover after going through the previous steps in this document. I am not going through on how to use these tools as there's plenty of documentation in Microsoft Technet about them.

4.0.7 Updates and Security patches

Ensure that the security patches and updates supplied by Microsoft and the application vendor get installed soon after they get released. You might need also to perform testing in UAT environments of your applications to ensure those don't break functionality.

If you think I can help you further in your quest to a secure IIS build I can be contacted @ the following website:

www.mitchjaloba.com

4.0.7   Updates and Security patches

Ensure that the security patches and updates supplied by Microsoft and the application vendor get installed soon after they get released. You might need also to perform testing in UAT environments of your applications to ensure those don't break functionality.

If you think I can help you further in your quest to a secure IIS build I can be contacted @ the following website:

www.mitchjaloba.com

Follow the instructions below to set:

    a.   In IIS manager select the site/application you want to apply it to and then select Request filtering and then edit Feature settings in the action pane.

In the General section uncheck Allow Double Escaping.

4.0.2   Dynamic IP restrictions (IIS8.x only)

IIS8.0 introduced this option which can be use to thwart DDOS attacks by blocking excessive repeated access attempts.

You need to add IP and Domain restrictions first. IIS can be configured to to deny access to websites based on the number of times that an HTTP client accesses the server within a specified time interval, or based on the number of concurrent connections from an HTTP client.

Please see the below URL where you can get step by step instructions on how to configure this feature:

https://www.iis.net/learn/get-started/whats-new-in-iis-8/iis-80-dynamic-ip-address-restrictions

4.0.3   HTTP Detailed Error Messages

Showing HTTP detailed error messages to display remotely can give clues as to how your IIS server is configured so it's best to disable it.

Please see the below URL to configure HTTP error messages to not display remotely:

https://www.iis.net/configreference/system.webserver/httperrors

While here you might as well ensure that custom Error messages are enabled.

4.0.4   IIS_IUSRS group and iiswasKey

By default only administrators and system should have access to this encryption key. In addition though IIS_IUSRS has access as well. This is a vulnerability and should be remediated.

For example you can use the below command from an elevated command prompt for .Net 4.0 64 bit:

%systemroot\Windows\Microsoft.NET\Framework64\v4.0.30319
\aspnet_regiis.exe -pr iisWasKey

4.0.5   Credentials in .config files

This is a vulnerability for IIS admin users credentials when stored in machine.config, root level web.config or application web.config files.

To remove please follow the instructions below:

a) Open the above config files and find the <credentials> section.
b) Remove the section

4.0.6   SCW and SCM

Use Security Configuration Wizard and Security Compliance Wizard to check the potential security pitfalls of your server leftover after going through the previous steps in this document. I am not going through on how to use these tools as there's plenty of documentation in Microsoft Technet about them.